Divide These

Divide These

Saskia Hamilton

Graywolf Press

Publication of this volume is made possible in part by a grant provided by the Minnesota State Arts Board, through an appropriation by the Minnesota State Legislature; a grant from the Wells Fargo Foundation Minnesota; and a grant from the National Endowment for the Arts, which believes that a great nation deserves great art. Significant support has also been provided by the Bush Foundation; Target and Mervyn's with support from the Target Foundation; the McKnight Foundation; and other generous contributions from foundations, corporations, and individuals. To these organizations and individuals we offer our heartfelt thanks.

A Jane Kenyon book, funded in part by the Estate of Jane Kenyon to support the ongoing careers of women poets published by Graywolf Press.

NATIONAL
ENDOWMENT
FOR THE ARTS

MINNESOTA
STATE ARTS BOARD

Published by Graywolf Press
212 Third Avenue North, Suite 485
Minneapolis, Minnesota 55401
All rights reserved.

www.graywolfpress.org

Published in the United States of America

ISBN 978-1-55597-422-0

Library of Congress Control Number: 2004116114

Cover design: Julie Metz

Cover art: Rogier van der Weyden, *Circle of Men Shoveling Chairs*
(or "Scupstoel"), ca. 1445–50.
The Metropolitan Museum of Art, Robert Lehman Collection, 1975. (1975.1.848)
Photograph © 1985 The Metropolitan Museum of Art

Contents

I

II

III

IV

for Joanna Picciotto

Where go the swallow tribes? the pathless main
Ne'er chronicles their flight

JOHN CLARE

I

The Weight of the Inside of the Body

It is a good thing to be in the vestibule.
The draft from the front door,
the hall lamp hanging from the ceiling, unlit,
the mind before it enters the house
of tenuous relationship, of starting,
of settling, of keeping still.

Year One

If the eyes move to the right: no.
If they stay in the center: yes.

The left is for listening because they sit
on the left side of the bed.

Only the eyes move. Someone
swabs her lips.

——

The first nurse is too cheerful.
The second does not know

how to speak to the speechless.
The third strokes her arm:

something settles down:
one lying, one sitting,

one in the doorway.

Listen

She undertook to collect him and carry his bones in such a way
that they might become reanimated.
Discussions with the children about the first
doctor and the last, vitamins and alternative medicines,
the visit when someone opened the cellar door
and someone else complained that he'd cleaned everything
and when she crouched down to pick them up again she
could not hold them in her arms, so she fetched a box
made from wood he had split last winter, or wanted
to split but didn't, it doesn't matter, the idea was to carry them
in such a way that they might be reanimated but who
could tell her if she had made a mistake.
Were the Christ collected and enchanted back,
or Eurydice following, or the man's
wife reassembling in the tale told by
the traveler from Greenland,
perhaps at last you would know.
The centipede distracts you. You sink;
the insects dig down, the mole digs forward.

Inside

First, there was the fifth mistake.
What you would take for the truth
was no longer supportable. Then came the dark
with its truncheon.
The table was trustworthy. It withstood
the trembling of the house
when the trucks passed and the road
broke some more. Dread
presaged the next thing, it is true
(but what it is not
is what it said); what it will not be
is what it said. One abstraction
muscles into another, without a system,
without a sound to sketch on paper except for these

instances and occasions: not even a half-hour piece;
a ten-minute piece, while the kettle is on the boil.

Year One

The pear in the bowl a week now.
Three days too long. The dark bruise
spreads and everything else
softens, as if in assent. The fifth
analysis, the sixth analysis
on the table. Still to be got to.
And alongside, the stacks of books
for the day to be got to,
the summer day, the winter day, the mind

sitting in the center of the body,
the body in the center of the house,
what pauses naturally,
what hesitates after
a comma and moves on.
Notice the breath caught
as if on a thorn in the thicket:
that is where your intelligence
is to be gathered.

One Wiser Says to the Other Unwiser

Jot this down:
if you favor your left shoulder, you are anxious.

If the right shoulder were to collapse,
the dead may have entered the muscle. They choose to persist,
or you choose to allow them to.

She Did Not Want to Hear Me Finish a Sentence

Because she was no longer present. Nor was he.
Because although you knew,
your body observing them go,
that their bodies emptying
might pass through
a dream or two, or the electrical wires,
no more illusion than illusion,
terminus than terminus—
You spoke to them, to yourself, but you
were not listening. Used the wrong
instrument for insight.

Printed Labyrinth

The morning bell going five, six, seven
before I lose count. Then quiet,

not a single engine, light on the building,
shadow on the road. This condition will last

as long as the longest sentence imaginable;
the one that will fill

two books before it rests:

The Labyrinth Suggests a Center

The past, however, is full of danger.
Black salt bowl on the table.

The lid, the spoon, a recurrent
undercurrent. The repetitions lead you from day

to day as from rock to rock and time
leads you forward toward

not the equinoctial line,
not the equinoctial road,

grief lengthens itself into the right shoulder
and reaches down.

Press it close to your sides and walk the crowded sidewalk,
as if the one were the other.

Year One

For what purpose were those hours poured
into the thimble?

You've gone from one day to the next,
below the measure.

The bright faces of flowers at night
where the path bends

to the left. Solitude, that is,
the irrelevance of the particular

person, the fact that does not matter.
The path was not one way it was any way.

Consider

Shovel some space in the narrow

between the road and field. The roots of grass
tangle your work. Two trees beside

the path. The white one
inside the forest of beeches.

The white one at dusk.

Inside

Records for the broken player.
No reason for order but order
persists, from breakfast to bath
to work, rain falling at one speed,
the windows darkening and blurring,
accident beating against belief.
A loud engine, which is one way to say
one thing. The floors swept daily,
though it takes at least one hour for the first,
one for the last. In the pages of a book,
quick studies of gesture,
tents of hands.

Then

Go on, go on, the other said.
Not not not, the other said. And I was not
listening, though it was all
I said, mid-morning, the tea
cold and the radiators finished with their sweet
ticking until four. The cold
was creeping back into the room, the not
was a creeper, a creeper I thought.

Not Known

Seventy lakes below.

The snow.

Houses at the edges.

The small airplane inches forward.

Salt on my fingers; a child waking one seat

back. Lakes have given way to fields.

No, not water; snow on the fields,

little squares and rectangles,

light glinting off the plane,

glinting off small rivers, travelling

forward like the rest of us from matter

to the account of matter. The boy

protests; he won't stop now until we land.

II

Precisions as to Place

Debris hits the building. The birds of the city
play on the updrafts, the undersides
of their wings white, or sooty,
or mottled, the mangy, the alert. Grit

and bits of asphalt.
Stacks of boxes on the pavement.
Wet faces of neighbors
climbing the stairs toward you as you

descend towards the mail.
The one you love
is the source of all quotation. His sentences
press into you. Two of his lines

sit in the drawer with its secret latch.
They have one length but they fit
and if the wing lengthened,
seven would become eight and therefore

holy, in a state of anticipation.
Pump the water from the earth,
bring it from the water table
to the surface,

but it seeps back
into the basement of the building.
There is a sixth one down there
with two broken teeth

and a soul of teeth; he will
last, he will be the last of us.
His father is proud.
You know the two I mean.

They were by the graves
like rows of teeth. It was
late in the dream
when dusk obscured the last

outline. The snow
on the tenth floor became rain
on the third. This snow
will never reach the pavement.

The mouth of the anemone
opens in stone. The minister
who spoke of it shone
a little brightly in his robes,

he did not care
that there was something
cheap in the fabric, he
was neither cheap

nor expensive. The fathers
sat by the well in their suits.
The wind blew their ties
and hit their bodies.

Below the ribs is where you store the breath. Ten jars along the floor.
Inside each,
dark, in-
decipherable design. If you listed fourteen instances you might make

a drawer for the missing so you could fold in-
side it *scriptio continua,* the stone flower, letters,

blue ladders on the scaffolding,
the scallion tables, fish so crowded
in the bin they don't move: turtles to rescue
from the bucket on the hammered

sidewalk slip down: step up
to the inside, empty from now
to the next commonwealth:
wherever we are we repeat ourselves:

or the alternative:
or the appearance of the god:
the hour: the old one: the mouth,
pared from rock and brought

here, that won't close again.

III

Canal

The visitors chatted about old cooks and dogs.
The figure on the bed in the front room:

the mouth ajar: the window ajar:
the drawbridge raised for the barge.

The Chair

If the chair were to be moved again,
it would find its own weight damaging. It
stands beside the chest. Its cloth
is worn away. Its brass fingers
keep a grip on things. Who would sit in it?
Who would read for a while beside it?

The Judge

The law functions now as window, as mirror, as
recorder. You won't read the work until later.

The chairs scrape. Those who have stayed in the room
whisper, they have stopped listening

to the body. Recall: the breath was caught,
the muscles conformed, the mind adjusted.

The breath leaving by one,
returning by two, leaving by one.

The broad table, the small lamp,
unlit.

Elegy

Candles by the feet.

If you were to stay indoors and delete.
If deletion were to occupy the space.

The lamp in the next room a jar of darkness sealed by the rim
of the apparatus.

It lights the table by the two windows
and the yellow folders of letters from someone to someone.

The faces in the class relaxed in the morning.

The faces in the class unreadable in the afternoon.

The white paint now gray, the surface of the water an even
iron encroached upon by shadow.

Now one must observe the other from the back of the chair.

Now the what and wherefore.

Entrance

Two men rolling trash toward the gate.
Return to your underground where you at least
made progress in the books.
He licks the type, each letter broken open
by his tongue. They might have been legible,
they might have made threats against
the illegible city. The rain spoke
its own language and kept on.
Pockets of breath in the house; doors
that may be walled behind the plaster.

Canal

The sluice opened, then closed.

The shipping was halted.
The muscle resists; you cannot move it.

Elegy

The work of burial is never done. First the interruption,
then the interruption, so it's carried on in sleep,
over to argument, floating in the water with the flowers
the shit the shells the debris from the city after the rains
have washed it to the beaches and the sea
has taken it up into itself. The figure with the shovel:
the figure with the shovel: the figure with
the book, the shoulders rising, the dog reading news
on the pavement washed then by rain running off the asphalt
down into the gulley where it goes under the city with the tunnelling

animals, the cunning animals, the readers under
the city.

Canal

So: the bridge was too low, which meant
this length was not for trade.
Your passengers must crouch in the center
of the hull. And your boat goes under

at the speed of walking.

Conspecifics

The train went on, one hundred and eighty minds
drifting all the way from Amsterdam

to Arnhem. The light moves from four-thirty
to five, then sinks for good: knocked off

early: we'll switch four times
before we stop: one face

closes up shop: one empties:
the storm that keeps almost coming:

faces facing themselves in the windows.

—–—

The filaments of sensation burn out:

one self chastises another self:
the labyrinth suggests a center:

the giant anteater stereotyping
from cage to pen to cage

and back again: the zoo
closing in an hour.

Dusk

Sound travelled to the nearby from the distant:

the wood pigeon following its own logic,
the farmer shooting crows.

The summer dusk

lifted the basin, the bar of soap,
the room in which the search

had once begun. The wasp searches

for the hole: the elusive moment, not still, un-
stillable, one going to the other.

Entrance

No one in the house but the two, the one
on the way to death, the other
on the way to earth. Above, the white sky, not ready
to rain, below, lush, the mid-summer garden,
the thrush, or the young of the thrush,
or the seventeenth generation thrush.

Below, a door opens. No one moves about
but you, in the white chair, typing.

Storm

Across the street, the park.
The wind lifts. What withdraws.
The dog on the line strains to get on with it.
The path hurries away.

Listen

       The shaded window.
Voices from the garden rose
to the room and soon the green blanket
soothed you. The phone rang. A door
closed. No one turning
down the gravel path, no one
taking up the garden shears.

Canal

Shoulders bowed round like the hull of the boat.
If the spine were to hold, you would float,

you would move toward the mouth,
you would not scuttle.

Entrance

Then I went indoors. First came the beautiful one, whose

only thought was to stop. Then came the beautiful one,

who lay in the grass. There followed the five beautiful ones

who took shovels and spades with them. Lastly,

there was you. You looked from the window. We said

the one no to each other that was required.

The ones that followed swept them up,

the two negatives. Open, open.

Entrance

If the hornets she crushed in the glass
were instead to gather in her hair.

If the textures of the wall in the sleeper's
vision were to stop changing and settle him back.

If the lamp were not to be lit for some days
while the inhabitants did other things but read
into the night.

If instead of or inside of or in place against
the site or the conflict.

Small sweetness. As if the bowl.
As if the spoon.

The letters had no voice but the one
sound made by the floor

he stands on.

Blessed is he who came into being
before he came into being.

IV

Divide These

The black gauze on the scaffolding.
Steady winter rain; softening rain.
You at lunch at the table with the five
chairs. You finished now and at your work,
the Sunday work. The Sunday
night approaches, that we might
wrestle. And then as each day clears
another away, what's to be counted on?
Only night   First light
Only night   First light

      I will not quite
      fit in this hole
      nor you with
      your long fingers

One by Two

The gray ridged bus, the reluctant engine, the sluggish
engine: who would have thought: we are

responsible for each other: we board at St.
Vincent's, from under the plexi shelter:

The rain outside observing you in passing:

the Russian sentences, the German sentences,
the Dutch and English paragraphs and lines:

In the museum, the painting of rain:
what window to look through:

outside, the storm blowing in
from the east: the city gray,

spotted with yellow and red lights
from marquees and windows:

They cut the flax and lay it in a ditch
for weeks: it did not rot,

it softened in the water:
they beat and beat it, then

the men spun it, splitting their fingers open:
and then, in spring, the weaver came,

stayed a week, going
from farm to farm:

In one film, a man turns the page of a book:
in another film, a man turns the page

of a book: the director moved
from continent to continent, he worked

in translation, but the one image
did not change: the man breathing,

the page turning, the weight of
the paper in his hand:

The reading room a place of prayer:
the subway platform a place of prayer:
so much silence in which to worry:

notice how long it takes to move through
the underworld: the bones of the ear
in the bones of the dead:

The invisibility of our messages,
passed along the old

transatlantic cable: you in your kitchen
in the half dark, my journey

from land to land by ferry:
as if to hear were to touch you:

hands do not act:
wish fastens the binding:

Everything grows damp,
the bags, the book jacket, thin film

of circumstance guiding the boat forward
toward the island in its place,

the heart in its moment, trust
drifting beyond the boundaries

of the story: the ferry
turns toward a light:

to come, to follow: the dry indoors:

High-rises with lifts near the parks,
geraniums on the balconies, and inside,
pensioners moving slowly:

all the local shops have shut down:
walk out the building:
the newspaperman now sells

onions, salt, potatoes, newspapers:
bicycles, engined
by young men in creased trousers,

go past:

After the journey from the farmhouse to the apartment house,
the difficulty of leasing, claiming, resolving disputes

is contemptible, the judge despises his little kerchief, the bickering,
that they stand before him, that

he is to turn judgment on a word:

The runner took it from the shelf and brought it,
wrapped in my request: the paper

was a note toward the definition:
the price less than a tenth

decimal point: a bribe
or reason, close investigation,

an instance of seeing without seeing:
the permission I sought

was pointless: auricular assurance:
the fox in stealth: the pacts, the underhand,

the not permitted, the concealed:

I went on a false journey, knowing
it was false, surrendering to

its insights while the first metaphor
could not be layered over

the second; do not be dutiful, do not
do as you are supposed to do:

the streets are now empty of strangers;
everyone is drawn inward,

the tram conductor keeps his counsel:

We reached the island on Saturday and stayed the night
while overhead jets passed,

startled the cattle:

In the new film, the subtitles blur the image:
but it is an old film: what is the same

anywhere in the world? A field:
trees at its edges: the figure

approaching us: what is the source
of the sound? The projector was whirring

but has since settled down:

Tell me what you read: in your sleep,
if the watcher is watching, something

slips out: the struggle for breath:
there won't ever be

enough: how it manifests
in ways you hide yourself:

The insight on its late arrival: you look
angry as you name it, angry that it's

precise, roused by its precision to an anger that
won't dissolve in your legs until you get up

and mark the page yourself:

If I stood for your arrival, I knew better
than I knew, going up the steps

saying name, name, as your taxi
pulled to the curb:

it was not known, it was not past
knowing: everything unreadable appeared

hidden afterwards but I read
of it in my sleep: images

worked their invisible way through: what:
through the honey: the berry on the tongue

that turned, shrugged: a bee:

We drove under the pilings: the starlings rose
and ducked behind the construction and were not

visible to us, only audible:

Hay wrapped in black plastic,
cups and sheeting by the tracks,

the strangely tense wait for what or why,

muser in sentences, intermittent rain,
musique concrète on the repaired record

player, what you haven't used,
couldn't use,

red poppies in the cut fields,
white butterflies by the tracks:

Something moves through the blood on its errand:
measure the breath and all

will be measured: swallows settle
on the power lines: raise

the flocks: come inside,
where the dead and their tribes

no longer need attending to:
the translation of *why* and *why not*

is tapped out one by two by one by two:
but you are alert to quiet movement:

bees hover low in the grass.

The lamp is lit.

Contingent Ends

The red shallot parting from itself
on the plate: the next day: my thought: you
waking at midnight to phone: the ceiling sloping over
the bath: the book: cold tea: spent bulb:
the dark room: the bright screen:

Notes & Acknowledgments

Listen [1]: "Reanimated": see Jerold Ramsey, *Reading the Fire: Images in the Traditional Indian Literatures of the Far West* (Lincoln: University of Nebraska Press, 1983) and Åke Holtkrantz, *The Native American Indian Orpheus Tradition* (Stockholm: Ethnographical Museum of Sweden, 1957).

Precisions as to Place: Title and "Wherever we are we repeat ourselves": in Freud, *The Psychopathology of Everyday Life* (New York: Penguin Modern Classics, 2002), pp. xxi and vii.

Entrance [4]: "Blessed is he . . .": The Gospel of Thomas, 19, trans. Thomas O. Lambdin, in *The Other Gospels: Non-Canonical Gospel Texts* (Philadelphia: The Westminster Press, 1982).

One by Two: For Paul. "Auricular assurance": *King Lear* 1:2; "fox in stealth": *King Lear* 3:4.

I am grateful to the editors of *Chicago Review, Colorado Review, Columbia Review, Electronic Poetry Review, Literary Imagination, Lyric, New Yorker, New York Times Book Review, Ploughshares, Pool, Post Road*, and *Salt*, in which earlier versions of these poems were printed.

SASKIA HAMILTON (1967–2023) was the author of four collections of poetry, *As for Dream*, *Divide These*, *Corridor*, and *All Souls*. She was the editor of several volumes of poetry and letters, including *The Letters of Robert Lowell*, and was the co-editor of *Words in Air: The Complete Correspondence between Elizabeth Bishop and Robert Lowell*. Her edition of *The Dolphin Letters, 1970–1979: Elizabeth Hardwick, Robert Lowell, and Their Circle* received the Pegasus Award for Poetry Criticism from the Poetry Foundation and the Morton N. Cohen Award for a Distinguished Edition of Letters from the Modern Language Association. She was also the recipient of an Arts and Letters Award in Literature from the American Academy of Arts and Letters. She taught for many years at Barnard College.

Divide These has been set in Adobe Caslon Pro, an open type version of a typeface originally designed by William Caslon sometime between 1720 and 1766. The Adobe version was drawn by Carol Twombly in 1989. Book design by Wendy Holdman. Composition by Stanton Publication Services, Inc.